Exploring Nature

If you are interested in the world of nature, here is the book for you. Exciting but simple projects help you to find out for yourself about its elements – the soil we all live on, the trees, flowers and other plants that grow in it, and the birds, butterflies and countless other small creatures that share our existence.

Projects are grouped together in sections, which give any necessary background information at the beginning. None requires any special equipment – just odds and ends that can be found around the average home – and you can either work right through the book or dip into those sections that interest you most. Either way, you should thoroughly enjoy yourself while finding out lots of interesting things, and at the end of it all you will be well on the way to becoming a real naturalist.

Derek Hall is a biologist, whose main interest is marine biology. He has contributed to a number of books and publications and is the author of *My World of Nature*, also published by Hamlyn.

Exploring Nature

Derek Hall

Illustrated by Tony Morris

Beaver Books

First published in 1978 by
The Hamlyn Publishing Group Limited
London · New York · Sydney · Toronto
Astronaut House, Feltham, Middlesex, England
Reprinted 1978

© Copyright Text Derek Hall 1978
© Copyright Illustrations
The Hamlyn Publishing Group Limited 1978
ISBN 0 600 36589 1

Printed in England by Cox & Wyman Limited
London, Reading and Fakenham
Set in Monotype Times New Roman

Contents

Introduction

This book has been written to enable children to undertake simple projects and experiments in nature. Of course, there is much to be learned by reading about nature in some of the enormous number of books that are available in libraries or at school, but the real excitement comes from actually studying living animals and plants.

Obviously it is better to study nature by looking at animals and plants in their natural surroundings, but this is not always possible, and in many instances simple, temporary habitats can be made at home instead. Thus, for example, a large glass jar containing a colony of ants becomes a 'window' that allows you to glimpse into their secret, underground world.

The particular projects selected for this book have been chosen because they are simple to understand and easy to perform, and yet provide hours of fascination. None of the projects involves spending a great deal of time or money. For most of the experiments common materials like jam-jars, pieces of wire, coloured paper and muslin are all that is needed. Where other materials are necessary, they can be purchased cheaply even if they are not to be found around the house. Similarly, the animals and plants needed are those that you can collect easily, such as earthworms and plant seeds.

The key to success with any experiment in nature is to understand why you are carrying out the experiment in the way that you are, and to help in this respect, each experiment or project has a small introductory section which will explain something of the principles involved.

All good naturalists make notes of their observations, for in this way results of different experiments can be compared. Therefore, whenever you undertake a project, have a notebook handy and jot down any interesting or unusual observations you make, as well as noting down the things you expect to see.

There is only room to suggest a few experiments in this small book, but as your understanding increases it should prompt you to carry out further experiments on your own.

Finally, and most important, remember that all animals and plants have their part to play in the balance of nature. Respect their way of life as you study it, for all creatures have a purpose, and even those that you never see are acting out their role and helping to enrich our world.

Ponds and Pondlife

Ponds are some of the most exciting places to study nature. There is something about a pond that makes everyone want to know what is going on beneath the surface. Of course, we do not always *need* to look below the water to see signs of life. In spring, you may see a duck proudly leading her newly-hatched ducklings along, teaching them how to fend for themselves. There may also be other kinds of activity – the 'sploop' as a fish takes an insect, or the beautiful dragonfly, gracefully hovering over the lily pads.

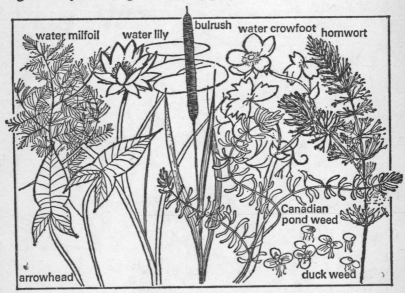

water milfoil   water lily   bulrush   water crowfoot   hornwort

Canadian pond weed

arrowhead

duck weed

Beneath the surface of the pond is a world teeming with life. Some of these forms of life are so small that you cannot see them without a microscope, but others, such as fish, beetles, worms and newts, are much easier to study.

In many places ponds are becoming spoilt due to man's interference with nature, and all good naturalists – young and old – should practise conservation. Study the animals and

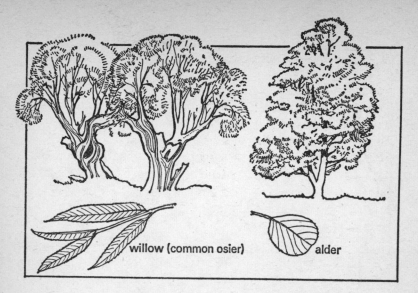

willow (common osier)   alder

plants, marvel at their way of life, but do not destroy it. If you do take a few animals, put them back alive when you have finished looking at them, and never take more than you really need. It is much more worthwhile to learn something interesting by studying a few selected animals than to put so many together that they would never behave in a natural way.

Mapping a pond

What you need
pencil
paper
coloured crayons
a long stick marked in metres
    and centimetres

This is best carried out in summer, when most of the flowers are in bloom. First, sketch the shape of the pond on the paper. Wherever trees, such as willow, grow near to the water's edge, mark them on the sketch. Mark also

11

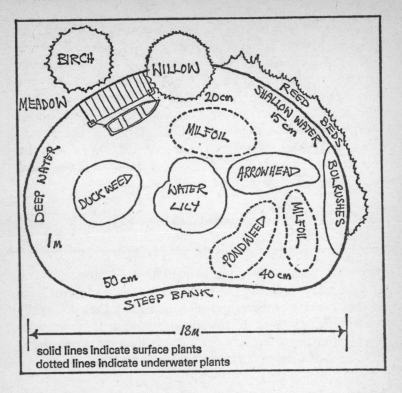

BIRCH

WILLOW

MEADOW

DEEP WATER

20cm

MILFOIL

SHALLOW WATER 15 cm

REED BEDS

BULRUSHES

DUCKWEED

WATER LILY

ARROWHEAD

1M

PONDWEED

MILFOIL

50 cm

40 cm

STEEP BANK.

|← 18m →|

solid lines indicate surface plants
dotted lines indicate underwater plants

steep banks, shallow banks and any man-made constructions such as a jetty. Using the pictures at the beginning of this section, try and identify as many water plants as you can find, and mark them on the map so that it shows their positions and extent. Some plants, like bulrushes, are rooted in the mud of the pond, but much of their stems are above water. Other plants, like milfoil, grow beneath the surface, but if you probe carefully with your stick you will be able to lift these clear of the water long enough for you to see what kinds they are. You can mark water lilies easily because their large, flat leaves float on the water. You will probably also see the much smaller leaves of duckweed which may occur anywhere since their roots just hang in the water. Now, using your depth-stick, measure the depth of the water around the edge of the pond and mark on your map any particularly deep or shallow areas. Do not try and measure the water too far away from the edge of the pond – you may fall in! You should now have an accurate picture of your pond. When you get home, re-draw it neatly using coloured crayons for the different plants. You can also make notes about which plants are in flower. Later in the year, revisit the pond with your map, and note any changes.

Making your own pond

What you need
an old fish tank or a
    large basin
jam-jars
a long handled net
pond water (or tap water)
small pond plants
pond animals

Making your own pond is great fun, and quite easy to do.
You can make it as elaborate or as simple as you wish, but
however you do it, if you bear the following hints in mind it
will prove to be a source of great interest and knowledge.

The sort of pond we are going to make here isn't the kind
you build in the garden because that usually involves lots of
digging, waterproofing and so on. Besides, it is very difficult
to see what goes on beneath the surface. You can make a
very simple pond from a shallow basin, but the best types are
made using old aquarium tanks. You may have one of these

in your loft – perhaps a leftover from when you once kept goldfish. If not, small, plastic tanks can be bought quite cheaply from pet shops or from the secondhand column of a local paper. Whatever you use to make your pond, the secret of success is to try and copy the conditions of a natural pond.

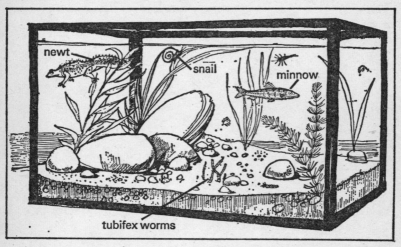

So first, cover the bottom of the tank with clean sand. Next, put in some stones (pond animals like to hide under stones). Now fill the tank with water. Pond water is best, but you can use tap water. You will need a few pond plants because, in addition to providing oxygen for the animals, they also serve as hiding places and will make the animals feel at home. Water milfoil, hornwort and pondweed are some of the best plants to use and you can find these by carefully searching in the pond with your net. To make your pond more like the real thing, sprinkle half a jam-jar full of fresh mud from the bottom of a natural pond into your tank. Don't worry if it suddenly looks all murky – the mud will soon settle to the bottom. Another advantage of this is that the eggs of some animals are often laid in the mud and sometimes creatures

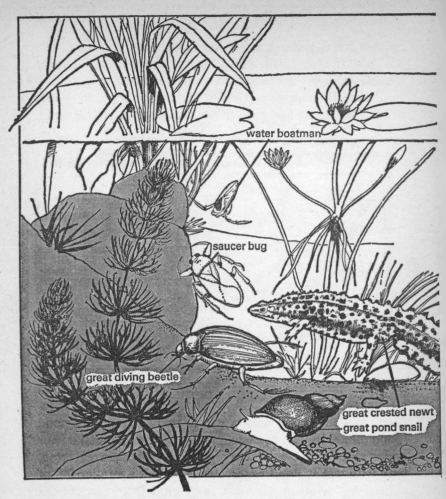

water boatman

saucer bug

great diving beetle

great crested newt
great pond snail

you never thought you had suddenly appear, having hatched out. Once the water has settled (it is best to leave tap water to stand for several days) you can start to think about the animals you want to put into your pond.

If you want to keep carnivorous (meat-eating) animals like diving beetles, dragonfly nymphs, water bugs and sticklebacks you should keep them individually, for unless your pond is very big, they will soon eat all the

stickleback

leech

freshwater shrimp

other animals. For a well-balanced pond a good selection to start with is snails, newts, caddis larvae, shrimps and tubifex worms. You can find most pond animals by carefully dipping into the pond in various places with your net. Carry the animals home in a jar full of water. Remember not to overcrowd the tank and to return any that you have finished looking at to the pond where you found them, to help preserve its natural stock.

Here are some of the things you may observe.

1. Snails rasping algae (tiny plants that look like little green dots) off the plants or off the sides of the tank with their *radulae* (horny tongues) to use for food.

great pond snail

2. Snails' eggs clinging to the weeds.
3. Swimming movements of shrimps.
4. Caddis larvae crawling about on the bottom in their protective tubes made of stones and twigs.
5. Hydra, a tiny green animal related to jellyfish, stretching and shortening its body, and waving its tentacles about looking for food.
6. Water beetles swimming, using their flattened legs which act like paddles.
7. Water beetles carrying a silvery bubble of air to breathe from under their wing cases.
8. Water beetles eating chopped worms that you put in the tank.

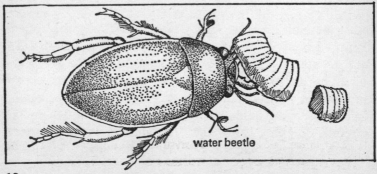

water beetle

9. Mating behaviour of sticklebacks. (You will need a small air pump if you keep sticklebacks for any length of time because they need plenty of oxygen).

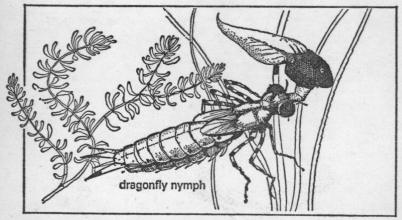

10. The 'mask' of a dragonfly nymph darting out to catch its prey, such as tadpoles, worms and small fish.

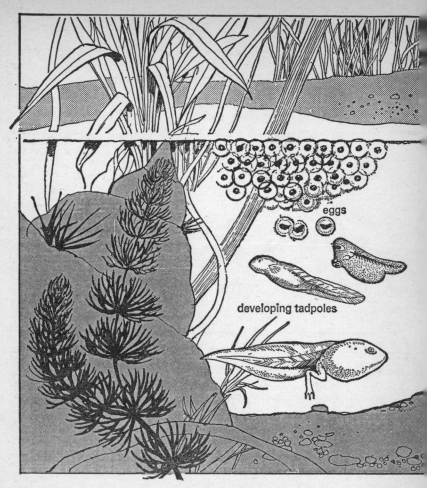

eggs

developing tadpoles

11. Metamorphosis (or development) of frogs. You can find frog spawn by the edges of ponds during spring. It looks like a mass of jelly with black dots (the eggs) in it. *Take no more than four or five eggs with their protective jelly to study.*

You will need to feed the carnivorous animals you keep, since they will not be able to find their natural food unless you put all the animals together, in which case, as already mentioned, some of them will soon be eaten. Mosquito larvae

frog

developing frog

(from the surface of the pond), live daphnia (water fleas from a petshop) and chopped worms make suitable food for most carnivorous pond animals. A magnifying glass is useful for studying the details of some of your animals and remember, a notebook with such observations as the date your tadpoles grew hind legs, the day they were ready to leave the water, the manner in which a dragonfly nymph seized its prey, will serve later as a useful reminder even if you do not keep your pond set up.

21

Bark and Leaf Rubbings

Have you ever looked closely at the bark of a tree? If you have, you will probably have noticed that it has a distinct pattern. It is marked by furrows, cracks, little pits and scars. What is even more interesting is that the bark pattern on one kind of tree – say an oak tree – is completely different from that of an apple tree or indeed from any other kind of tree. Bark patterns are one of the things that botanists (people who study plants) use to help them identify trees.

Leaves are another part of the tree that are useful for telling us what type of tree it is for they, too, have a pattern and shape which is unlike that of any other tree. What other parts of the tree might you look at for identification?

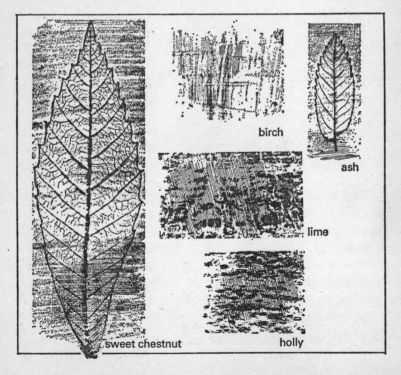

birch

ash

lime

sweet chestnut

holly

Making bark rubbings

What you need
some thick white paper
a soft lead pencil or
    dark crayon

All you need to do to make a bark rubbing is hold a piece of paper against the bark and go over the paper with the side of the pencil or crayon. As you do this, the pattern of the bark will begin to appear on the paper. When you are satisfied with your print write the name of the tree on the paper (you may already know the tree but if not, your library will probably have books to help you) and mark the paper with an arrow to indicate the right way up. Repeat this on several different trees using fresh paper each time and compare the bark patterns.

Making leaf rubbings

What you need
some thin white paper
a soft lead pencil or
    dark crayon
some fresh leaves

If you hold a leaf up and look through it, you can see a series of lines going along, and sometimes across, the leaf. These are the *veins*, which are really tubes through which water passes. If you feel the underside of the leaf you will feel the veins, or the larger ones at least, as ridges.

Place the leaf with its underside uppermost. Lay the paper over the leaf and go over it with the pencil or crayon as you did with the bark print.

Displaying your leaf and bark rubbings

What you need
scissors
paste or glue
stiff board

The best way of displaying your leaf and bark rubbings is to trim off the paper with scissors and then to stick them on to the stiff board, printing or writing neatly underneath each one the common name and, to make your display even more valuable, the scientific name as well.

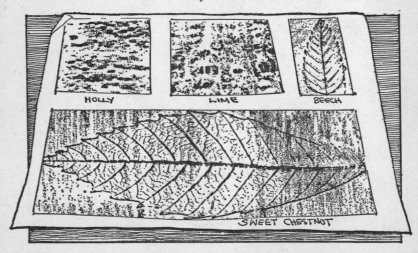

HOLLY   LIME   BEECH

SWEET CHESTNUT

Investigating Soil

Of all the places which support life, soil is one of the most interesting. Yet, because it is the world literally beneath our feet, it is often overlooked. But just think what lives in the soil. All the trees and flowers need soil in which to grow, and animals large and small burrow into it for shelter or to find food. A bucketful of typical soil will usually be found to contain worms, insects, mites, plant roots and seeds, plus an enormous variety of other minute creatures.

You may have noticed that not all soil looks alike. Some kinds are light in colour, others are dark. Again, some are crumbly and others seem almost sticky. This is because although most soils are made up of the same things – the soil constituents – the amounts of each vary.

Soil is made up of the following: **stones** – large particles formed from rock; **sand** – smaller particles formed from rock; **clay** – small particles formed from rock; **humus** – decaying animal and plant remains; **dissolved minerals** – the chemicals which are necessary for the healthy growth of plants; **bacteria** – tiny organisms that help turn the humus into minerals; **water** and **air**.

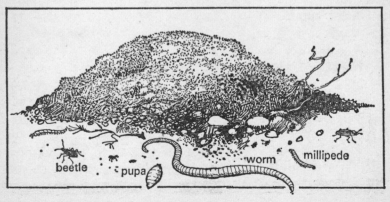

beetle pupa worm millipede

Separating soil into its constituents

What you need
a milk bottle
some soil
water

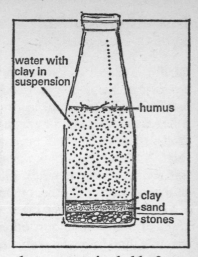

water with clay in suspension

humus

clay
sand
stones

Fill the milk bottle with about 4 cm of soil, and add water until it is 10cm from the top of the bottle. With your hand over the open end, shake the bottle until all the soil has mixed with the water, then leave it to settle. Because the heaviest particles sink fastest, the soil will separate into distinct layers. When a typical garden soil is treated in this way you can see at once the amount of stony particles compared to sandy particles, and the amount of sandy particles compared to clay particles.

Where there is a large amount of clay in the soil, it is called a *heavy* soil, and its particles are very small and close together. This means that water is held for a longer time than it would be in a soil with particles which were less close together. Heavy soils also have little air in them. Why do you think that is?

If a soil contains a large amount of sand, it is called a *light* soil. Here, the particles are larger and although there is more air, the water sometimes drains away too fast, washing away the valuable minerals as it does so. A soil with a mixture of sandy and clay particles is called a *loam*.

You could repeat this project using equal volumes of soils that you think might have different clay and sand contents and compare them.

How water drains through sand and clay

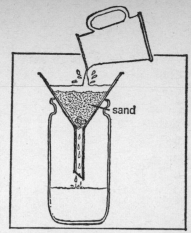

What you need
a plastic funnel
cottonwool
a jam-jar
sand
clay
water

You will need a fairly large plastic funnel for this project. Perhaps your mother has an old one in the kitchen that you can use. If not, they can be bought very cheaply in hardware shops.

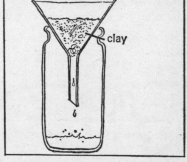

Place the funnel in the jam-jar so it is well clear of the bottom. If the funnel is too long, cut a hole in a piece of cardboard and rest it in this first. Plug the funnel with cotton wool. Now put a measured amount of sand in the funnel and pour on an exact volume of water – ⅓ pint or 200 ml. Note how long it takes for all the water to drain into the jam-jar. Now empty all the water out of the jam-jar, tip away the sand, clean the funnel and plug it as before with a fresh piece of cotton-wool of the same size. Using a volume of clay equal to the volume of sand that you used originally, and the same amount of water, record how long it takes for the water to drain through the clay. Do the results you obtain agree with what you read to start with about the properties of light and heavy soils?

The tiny animals in soil

What you need

mutton cloth or fine mesh gauze

cardboard

adhesive tape

a reading lamp

a magnifying glass or hand lens

soil and leaf litter

a tin can without the top and bottom*

a dish (to collect the animals in)

*It is best if an adult removes the top and bottom for you.

Most soils are full of tiny animals, but even if you search through a sample of soil by hand you would be bound to miss quite a few. What we shall do in this project is set up a lamp over a sample of soil. This dries the soil and the animals crawl downwards, away from the heat to where the soil is still moist. Eventually they crawl right to the bottom, fall through a mesh and can be collected in the dish and examined.

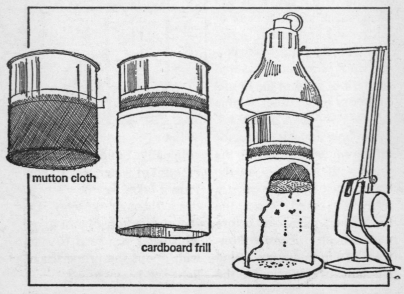

mutton cloth

cardboard frill

Stretch some mutton cloth over one open end of the tin can (try and use a can that has a diameter of at least 10 cm) and tape it in place. Now cut some cardboard to make a frill about 12 cm deep. Tape this securely to the bottom of the can, and place the can and frill in the dish. Put some fresh soil and leaf litter in the can and set up the lamp so that it rests just in the top. Try not to use a lamp stronger than 40 watts. If you have to use a more powerful lamp, position it further away. Very soon the first animals, irritated by the heat, will have fallen into the dish. Make a list of all the different kinds you find – centipedes, worms, slugs, insects – and put them back outside after you have examined them. It may take a few days for the smallest animals to fall through, and the kindest method is to look under the frill from time to time and identify and release any animals you find.

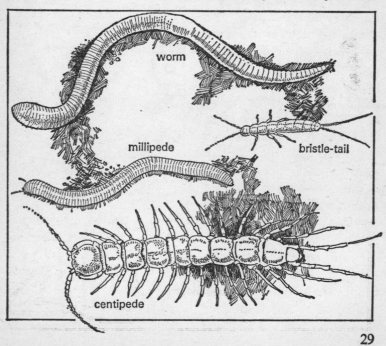

worm

millipede

bristle-tail

centipede

Trapping animals on the soil surface

What you need
an opened tin can
a skewer
a tin lid

4 long cocktail sticks
a small piece of meat or fruit

The excitement of this project is that you can lay the trap wherever you like and, having examined and released the animals, you can set it up again somewhere else. You can never be sure what will fall into the trap – which adds to the fun!

First, ask a grown-up to make a small hole in the bottom of the can with the skewer. This allows any water to drain out and prevents the animals drowning. Dig out a small area of soil and push the can in so that it is level with the top of the hole, replacing the earth around the edges. You can place a small piece of meat or fruit in the can to act as bait. Now make a canopy using the four sticks and the tin lid. This will help prevent rain coming in, and will keep the sun off the animals. Many small animals such as beetles are active at night, so you could set the trap up at dusk and inspect it the next

day. Do not be discouraged if you do not catch any animals at your first attempt, although you may of course be lucky at your first try. Remember to let your catch go after you have studied it.

Hatching soil pupae

What you need
screw-cap jar with breathing
   holes in the lid
soil
soil pupae

Many insects lay their eggs in the soil. These develop into larvae, which feed on the animals and plants in the soil, and in time, the larvae turn into *pupae*. This is a stage between the larval form and the adult. You may often come across pupae whilst looking in the soil; they are usually cigar-shaped, often dark red or brown in colour, and may vary in length depending on the type of insect into which they will develop. They are not usually longer than 3 cm.

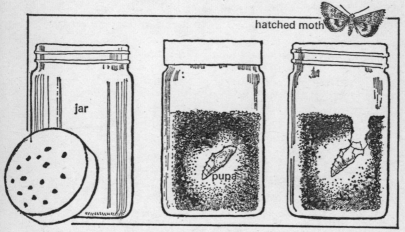

hatched moth

jar

pupa

If you find some pupae, put them in some soil in the jar, replace the lid and wait for them to hatch into adults. Beetle and moth pupae are often found in soil. Another good place to look for beetle pupae is around rotting tree stumps, which provide good hiding places for the larvae.

Looking at Earthworms

Most of us have seen and know what an earthworm looks like. A few digs into the soil with a garden spade will usually produce several – unless the soil is very dry when they will have burrowed quite deeply underground. Perhaps it is because they are so common that they are often ignored, but nevertheless many interesting experiments can be done with them.

Earthworms belong to a group of animals called *annelids*, which have bodies divided into compartments called segments. Leeches and many of the worms to be found at the seaside, such as fan-worms and lugworms, are also annelids. Look at an earthworm and you will see at once that it has no true head and no legs. Near the front of its body is the mouth. Earthworms eat leaves and tiny particles of humus in the soil. Sometimes they actually eat their way through the soil, passing unwanted soil out at the other end, often leaving worm casts.

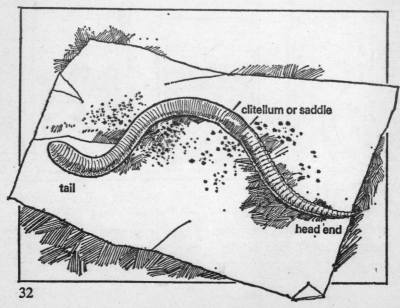

clitellum or saddle

tail

head end

What kind of soil do earthworms like best?

What you need
a bucket, or some sheets
   of newspaper
a spade

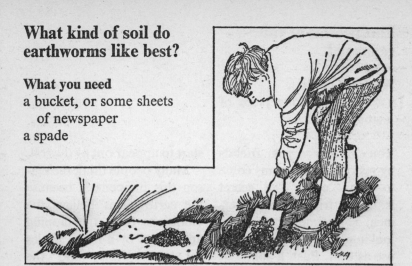

For this, choose a day that is neither too hot nor too cold, preferably after rain. Mark out an area about 50 cm square, and dig out the soil to a depth of about 30 cm. Place it all in a bucket or on a few sheets of newspaper and then carefully search through the soil, replacing it in the hole as you do so, and count every worm you find. Note the number to compare it with that of the next patch.

Now repeat the experiment using different soils. If you chose a sandy soil first, compare the number of earthworms that you find in a similar volume of clay soil, stony soil and the sort of soil you find on a broad-leaved woodland floor. You will find that certain soils have more earthworms than others, and the types of soil they prefer are those that allow them to move easily and that provide plenty of food for them. Why do you think that earthworms are often found under compost heaps?

Another way of collecting worms from a particular soil is to pour a strong solution of washing-up liquid and water on to the soil. The worms will soon emerge.

Earthworms at your command

What you need
a spade or a long piece of
stout wood

You can amaze your friends by making earthworms come to your 'call'. The secret is an old trick which fishermen sometimes use when looking for earthworms to use as bait. Push a spade or a flat piece of wood into damp soil at an angle and tap it several times. In a few minutes, earthworms will start to appear out of the soil.

Many people think the reason this happens is because the earthworms believe the vibrations from the tapping are caused by a mole. Moles eat earthworms, and the earthworms leave the safety of their dark, underground world in order to escape being eaten.

How earthworms mix soil

What you need

a jam-jar
soil
sand
brown paper

an elastic band
a few small leaves
some earthworms

Earthworms are truly the farmer's friend, for their constant burrowing through the soil helps put air into it and mix together all the minerals that plants need for healthy growth.

To show how earthworms mix soil, fill a jam-jar with alternate layers of soil and sand, making each layer as level as you can. You can flatten the soil down with a wine glass base or a small tin bottle top nailed to a piece of dowelling. Cover the outside of the jar with dark paper. Place a few small leaves on top of the final layer, and put four or five earthworms on top of the leaves. Keep the jar in a cool place and moisten the top of the soil with a few drops of water every few days. After a week or so remove the dark paper and look at your jar. The earthworms' burrowing will have mixed up the sand and soil, and they will have dragged the leaves below the surface. In time the leaves will rot to provide food.

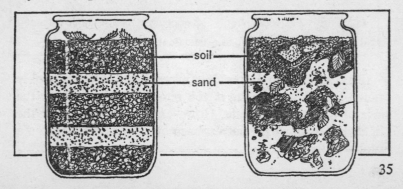

soil

sand

How earthworms move

What you need
a jam-jar
a smaller jar to fit inside the
  jam-jar
soil
some earthworms

We know that earthworms have no legs, so how *do* they move? The way they move is extremely interesting and well worth studying. The stages of movement are shown below.

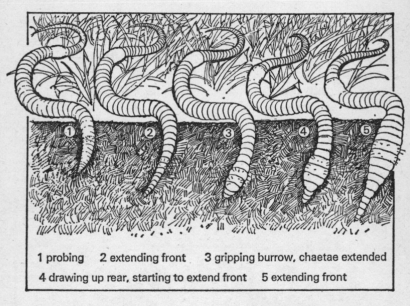

1 probing   2 extending front   3 gripping burrow, chaetae extended
4 drawing up rear, starting to extend front   5 extending front

If you have set up the previous experiment you can probably watch the worms moving if you remove the paper from the side of the jar for a while. However, because they shun the light, the earthworms may soon move out of sight into the centre of the jar.

The best way to watch earthworms moving is to set up another glass jar with a smaller jar inside it, leaving a space of about 2 cm between them. Pour soil into the gap between the jars and then put a few earthworms into the soil. In this way they will not be able to burrow away from view.

Beneath the skin of an earthworm are layers of muscle. Some layers run down the length of the body allowing it to shorten, and others run around the girth of the body allowing it to stretch. Watch how the earthworm probes about in the soil first, feeling for a gap. Then it pushes the front part of its body forward and grips the sides of the burrow with tiny rods called *chaetae* which it can draw in and out of its segments. The front part of the body now fattens, also helping to grip the burrow. Having done this, it uses its muscles to pull the rest of the body forward.

If you place an earthworm on a piece of stiff paper you can see and hear the chaetae. As the worm wriggles, the chaetae rasp against the paper surface.

Seaweed Pictures

Most rocky seashores have a large variety of seaweeds growing on them, and specimens can easily be collected and preserved to make attractive and informative decorations.

Seaweeds are usually grouped, or *classified*, according to their colour. Although all seaweeds contain the green pigment chlorophyll just as other green plants do, sometimes this green colour is masked by the presence of other pigments so that some seaweeds appear brown and others appear red.

Next time you go down to a rocky shore, collect a few different coloured seaweeds to make seaweed pictures when you go home. You may be one of those lucky people who live near the sea and can visit it when you like, but if not, collect a few seaweeds on the last day of your holiday and carry them back inside a sealed plastic bag with a little sea water.

What you need

a large flat dish

some strong white paper

a paintbrush

an old stocking or leg of a pair of tights

blotting paper

cardboard or a small piece of hardboard

some heavy books to use as weights

some seaweeds

What types of seaweed should you collect? Do not collect any that are *too* large because you will need to stick them on to the paper. About half-way down the seashore you will find the brown seaweed called *Fucus serratus*. This is a good seaweed to choose for one of your pictures. Further down, you may find the red seaweed *Rhodymenia palmata*. Some of the most attractive pictures are made using the more delicate seaweeds – look for *Bryopsis plumosa* (a green seaweed) in rock pools. Many of the beautiful red seaweeds grow on the rocks below the low tide mark, but these often get washed up with the tide so always look out for them. Of course, the few seaweeds mentioned here are only a guide, you will probably have your own favourite kinds.

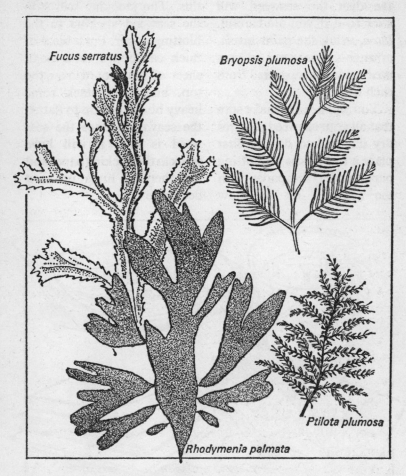

Fucus serratus

Bryopsis plumosa

Ptilota plumosa

Rhodymenia palmata

To make a seaweed picture using one of the less delicate varieties such as *Fucus*, first wash the seaweed and lay it on a sheet of paper. For the more delicate kinds such as the *Ptilota* shown in the picture, float the seaweed in a dish of water and then slide a sheet of paper underneath it. As you draw the paper out of the dish the seaweed will stick to it if you are careful. Now, using the paint brush, arrange the seaweed so that the fronds are separated from each other.

You will need to make sure that all your seaweed pictures dry flat and to do this first place a few pieces of blotting paper under the paper with the seaweed on it. Now place a piece of stocking over the seaweed and then put some blotting paper over this. The stocking will stop the seaweed sticking to the blotting paper. Put a piece of thick cardboard or a small sheet of hardboard over the top, and then stack some heavy books on top to flatten the seaweed. Once the seaweed is dry, it will have stuck to the backing paper and can then be hung up as a decoration.

Fungi

Fungi are a curious group of plants. Because they do not have the green pigment called chlorophyll they cannot make their own food in the way that green plants can. Green plants use chlorophyll to trap the energy produced by sunlight, and this energy is then used to combine water and carbon dioxide (present as a gas in the air) to make sugar. Because fungi have no chlorophyll, they therefore have no need of sunlight. This is why they are usually found in shady places – under trees, nestling among grass or growing on the side of rotting tree trunks. Fungi obtain their food by absorbing the juices of dead or living plants and animals. Those that feed on living material are called *parasitic*, whilst those that live on dead or decaying matter are called *saprophytic*.

During late summer or early autumn, when it is still quite warm but the weather is becoming damper, *fruiting bodies* begin to appear. These are the parts of a fungus with which we are most familiar – the mushrooms and toadstools. For most of the year, however, the fungus exists underground, or among the tissues of whatever it is living on, as a mass of thin threads called a *mycelium*.

Beneath the cap of a fungus are thin folds called *gills* or, in some kinds of fungi, tiny tubes are found instead. In these gills or tubes are formed the spores, which are shed to be carried by the wind and eventually form new fungi.

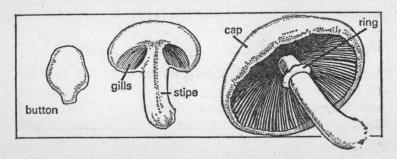

Spore prints from fungi

What you need
a sheet of white paper
a mushroom or toadstool

To make a spore print, carefully detach the cap from the
stalk or *stipe* (they usually
break quite cleanly) and,
taking care not to damage the
delicate gills, place the cap
gills downward on to a sheet
of clean white paper. After a
day, many spores will have
fallen from the gills and left a
clear pattern – the spore
print – on the paper. Not all
spores are the same colour, so
try making spore prints with
various kinds of fungi and see
what differences there are.
To preserve your spore print,
spray it with a clear varnish.

a jam-jar may be placed over the mushroom

Try and identify the fungi you use – your local library will
probably have a guide to common fungi – and write the name
underneath the spore print. Remember that some fungi are
poisonous, so always wash your hands after handling any.

Studying fungi

Fungi are much simpler plants than trees or flowers, but they
still make very interesting objects for study. Have you ever
noticed how fungi seem to spring up overnight? What looked
like a patch of bare ground yesterday may be covered with

mushrooms or toadstools today. The fruiting bodies grow very quickly. Sometimes you can see them just before the gills are exposed, when they are called *buttons*. Choose a particular young mushroom or toadstool to study and record how long it takes to become ripe and then shrivel away after all the spores are shed.

Have you noticed how the stipe of a mushroom or toadstool always bends if it is growing at an angle so that the cap is always horizontal? This is so that the spores always drop vertically and do not get trapped on the gills, for if they became trapped they would be wasted.

Sometimes you may see a 'fairy ring' of mushrooms or toadstools. This is caused by the mycelium radiating outwards from a central underground point and sprouting fruiting bodies.

If you walk in a meadow in summer you may see puff balls. These are fungi which produce spores in a kind of sac instead of in gills or tubes. Tap the sac gently and a cloud of yellow spores will come out. It only needs a rain drop to splash on to the sac to send thousands of these spores into the air.

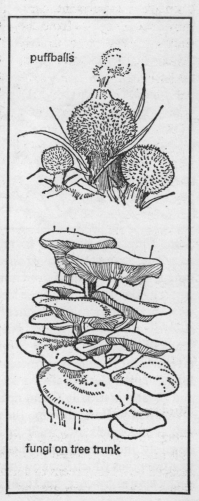

puffballs

fungi on tree trunk

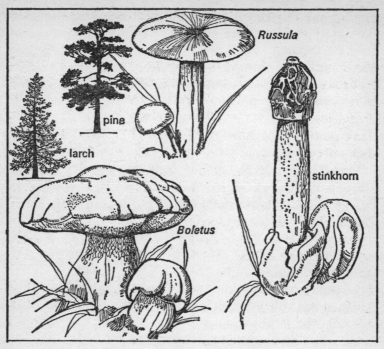

Some fungi always seem to grow beneath certain kinds of tree. These are called *mycorrhizal* fungi. The mycelium of the fungus spreads around, and sometimes into, the root of the tree and absorbs some of the tree's food products. The tree in turn obtains minerals and water from the fungus. This relationship, where both partners benefit, is called *symbiosis*. Some kinds of tree cannot grow properly unless the right kind of mycorrhizal fungus is growing with them. For example, the fungus called *Russula* always seems to grow next to pine trees, and *Boletus* is usually found near larch.

If, when walking through the woods you notice an unpleasant, foetid smell and walk in its direction you will almost certainly find a stinkhorn. This strange fungus emits the smell to attract flies which land on the top of it and help disperse the sticky spores by carrying them away on their bodies.

Invisible Spores in the Air

Stand outside and look into the air. What can you see? Perhaps you may see an insect flying past, or a bird. What you will not see are the millions of tiny fungal *spores*, nor the minute organisms called *bacteria*, that are always present in the air. They are not really invisible, of course, but they are so small that you need a microscope to see them.

We saw earlier how a fungus sheds millions of spores into the air to be blown away by the wind, sometimes to be carried for several kilometres. This helps the fungus colonise new areas. When the spores land in a suitable place, perhaps on a woodland floor, they germinate and grow to form a new plant. Of course, many fall in places where they cannot grow, such as on stony paths or in water.

What we shall do in these experiments is provide a suitable 'growing place' for some kinds of fungi and also for bacteria, and see firstly how long they take to grow, and secondly whether different places have different spores.

Growing fungi on bread and orange peel

What you need
2 saucers
2 tumblers
a magnifying glass
water
a piece of stale bread
a piece of orange peel

Place a few small pieces of the stale bread on a clean, dry

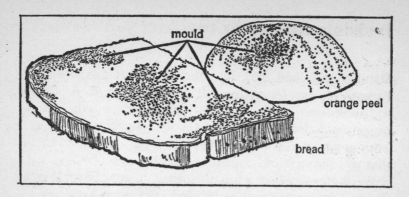

mould

orange peel

bread

saucer and *moisten* them with a few drops of water. Now place the tumbler over the bread so that it is completely enclosed. In a similar way, place a few small pieces of orange peel – also dampened – on the second saucer and cover that with the other tumbler. Try not to handle the bread and orange peel more than you have to.

After several days, you will see dark-coloured patches beginning to appear on the bread and orange peel. This is the start of your fungal colony. Are the fungus colonies more than one colour? Usually a green colony appears. This is *Penicillium* from which we get the drug penicillin. If you have a darker colony growing

it is probably *Rhizopus*. If it is white with black dots in it, it is probably *Mucor*. The colonies will continue to grow until all the goodness has been taken from the bread and orange peel. If you look at the colonies with a magnifying glass or a hand lens, you may be able to see that they are made up of thin strands. These strands together form the mycelium.

You could also set up what is known as a *control* experiment. This uses very dry bread or orange peel placed under separate tumblers. No fungi will grow on very dry food, showing that although the spores are always present in the air, they need moisture before they will start to form a mycelium.

Bacteria in the air

What you need
a culture medium (see below
 for details of how to make
 this)
4 small dishes with closely
 fitting lids

First, you must make up the
culture medium for the bacteria to grow on. To do this,
mix together 5g of malt
extract containing sugar, 1g
of meat extract (such as a
stock cube), a few drops of
orange juice and 20g of
gelatine in 160ml of water.
Heat this *gently* in a saucepan
and give it a stir until it all
dissolves. Pour an equal
amount of the culture

medium into each of the
dishes, and immediately cover
the dishes until the medium
sets. You should use dishes
and lids which are as clean as
possible, as this will help to
reduce the number of spores
already on the dishes. By far
the best way to ensure the
dishes are free from spores is
to use specially cleaned, or
sterile, *petri dishes* (small,
shallow plastic dishes with

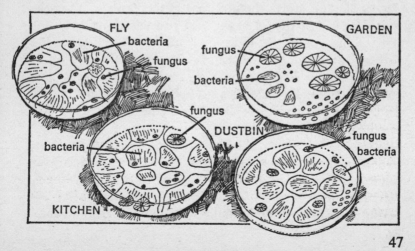

lids, which can be bought in sealed packs from laboratory suppliers), but even without these the experiment will still work well if you are careful. Any closely fitting lid will help to keep spores from the air off the dishes until you are ready to use them.

To compare the spores present in the air in different places, remove the lids from the dishes and put each dish in a different place; for instance, you could leave one near a dustbin, one outside in the open air and one in the kitchen. For the last dish, catch a fly and put it on the medium (put the lid back on to stop it escaping), and allow it to walk over the medium for a few minutes before releasing it. Put the lid back on the dish. After an hour, collect up the other three dishes, put their lids back on, and then leave all four dishes in a warm place, such as an airing cupboard. Without removing the lids, inspect them for the first signs of bacterial growth. These usually look like circular patches dotted over the surface of the medium. Note how quickly the patches enlarge as the bacteria colonies grow, and compare the number of colonies on each dish. You may also find colonies of hairy fungi. On the previous page are the results of an experiment carried out by the method described above. Notice that few fungi spores are present in the shed where the dustbin was kept, but plenty of bacteria were present. Also, there are more fungi spores on the medium left in the garden. What else can you tell about spores in the air by looking at the illustration? If you want to try another experiment, place a hair on a fresh dish of culture medium.

As soon as you have finished any experiments using these culture plates you should scrape the contents of the plates out on to old newspapers and burn them; or you can pour strong disinfectant on to the plates first to kill off the bacteria. Always wash the dishes very thoroughly before using them again.

Secrets of the Gall

You may have already seen some plant galls, but not realised what they were. They often occur on oak trees and are sometimes called 'oak apples' although they have nothing to do with the true fruit of an oak tree, the acorn. Other types of oak gall occur on the leaves, but these are flatter and smaller than oak apples.

Galls also occur on other plants such as birch and willow trees, ivy, and rose bushes, to mention just a few. But what exactly are galls, and how are they formed? Certain insects lay their eggs in the tissues of plants, and they do this by drilling a tiny hole in, say, a leaf, and then inserting an egg. The plant reacts to this intrusion by enveloping the egg in a hard, swollen case. This case is the gall. Thus oak galls are produced by the oak tree as a reaction to the egg-laying activities of an insect – in this case the insect is the gall wasp. Small insects called aphids also cause plants to produce galls, and so do certain mites, which are tiny animals related to spiders.

Looking inside an oak gall

What you need
a sharp knife
a twig containing an oak gall

Collect a few galls in early summer (about May) and carefully cut one open. Inside, you will find the developing gall wasp which will probably be in the larval stage.

Hatching a gall wasp

What you need

a screw-top jar with a hole drilled in the lid
water
an elastic band

pieces of thin wire
some butchers' mutton cloth
some oak galls on twigs

Get an adult to make a hole in the jar lid, fill the jar with water and then push the cut ends of the twigs through the hole in the lid and screw it on. (You can use a jam-jar and a cardboard disc with a hole cut in it if you do not have a screw-top jar.) Now bend the wire to make a frame over the twigs, and cover the frame with the mutton cloth, securing the top end with the elastic band. The water will keep the twigs fresh and the mutton cloth will prevent the gall wasp escaping once it hatches out. Watch every day for the appearance of the black gall wasp and once you have studied it, undo the mutton cloth and let it go.

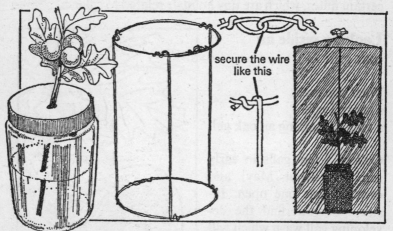

secure the wire like this

You can repeat the experiment using other plants which you suspect have galls on them, and see what hatches out.

Rearing Butterflies and Moths

Butterflies and moths make up the group of insects called the *Lepidoptera*. Although butterflies and moths are quite similar in many ways, they can usually be told apart by remembering the following: butterflies usually fly by day, have antennae with knobs on the end, and most of them fold their wings upward when resting; moths tend to fly at dusk or at night, usually have feathery antennae, and often fold their wings flat when resting.

Moths and butterflies both have a similar life cycle. The female lays her eggs – usually, but not always, on plants – and the larva (caterpillar) hatches out to feed on the plant. In time, the larva turns into a pupa (chrysalis). Unlike the active larval stage, the pupal stage is a sort of resting period. Eventually, the pupa splits open to reveal the adult insect that has been developing within.

Although many people collect the eggs of butterflies and moths and watch them hatch into caterpillars, they are often harder to find than the caterpillars and sometimes you have to wait a long time for them to hatch. Therefore it is better to collect a few caterpillars and watch them pupate and turn into adults.

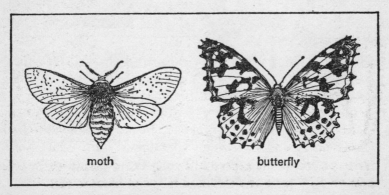

moth   butterfly

What you need

a jam-jar

a porous pot containing
  fresh soil

some thin wire

some muslin

water

a few caterpillars and their
  food plant

Many caterpillars are very much like their food plant in colour.
This is a method of protecting themselves from being eaten by
predators such as birds, but it also means that you may have to
look carefully to find them. Spring and early summer are the
best times to look for caterpillars. Look for them on the leaves
and stems of small bushes and other plants such as nettle and
privet.

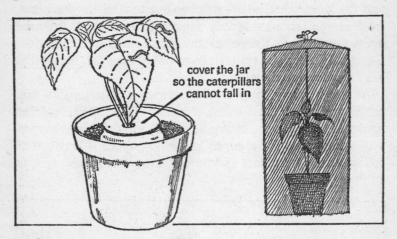

cover the jar
so the caterpillars
cannot fall in

Before you bring back any
caterpillars, prepare a cage
to keep them in. All you need
for this are two loops of wire
joined by straight pieces of
wire as shown, and a covering
of muslin. Make sure that any
ends of wire are outside the

cage, so that when the adult
insects emerge they will not
damage their wings.

Fill the jam-jar with water
and push it into the pot
containing soil. When you
bring the caterpillars home
on their food plant, place

the stems in the jar of water and cover it with the muslin cage. The caterpillars will only feed on fresh food plants, so when their food begins to wither put them on some new pieces of plant. If you do not want to handle the caterpillars, just place the new plant alongside and they will crawl over by themselves.

In time the caterpillars will stop feeding. If they are moth larvae they will probably pupate in the soil, but butterfly pupae will pupate on the food plant or on the muslin. Do not disturb them at this stage. If you watch the cage often enough, you may witness the emergence of an adult from its pupal case. Use one of the many books available on the identification of butterflies and moths if you have not already identified the insect from the caterpillar. You should release any adult insects as soon as possible, because they need to feed on the nectar of flowers.

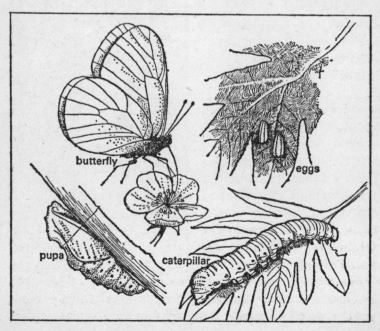

Attracting Moths

You can often see butterflies in the daytime, hovering from flower to flower. Moths, however, are usually active at dusk or at night, so to see them, you have to attract them in some way. There are several ways of attracting moths: you can leave a food source for them to come to, or make a light box (moths and many other night-flying insects are attracted by light), and some people even hang a female moth in a bottle and wait for her to attract males into the bottle by her scent!

Attracting moths with food

What you need

treacle	saucepan
a little beer	white paper
sugar	pins
a little rum	

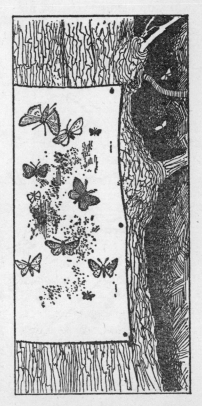

Choose a warm, overcast, windless night to do this project. To make up the food mixture, mix two tablespoonfuls of treacle with about four tablespoonfuls of sugar and heat the mixture, stirring it gently, until the sugar dissolves. Now add a little beer and a few drops of rum. (You will have to ask your parents for these last two ingredients!) Instead of beer, you can use cider if you wish.

Just before dusk, pin a piece of white paper to the side of a tree or fence and smear some of your food mixture near to it. The paper will help the insects find the food, but they will probably be drawn to it by the sweet smell anyway. If you are lucky you may soon find your food mixture completely covered by moths and other night-flying insects, all jostling with one another to have a drink.

Attracting moths by light

What you need

a wooden box
a strong (at least 60w)
    light bulb
a lamp holder
flex
a plug
adhesive tape
2 pieces of glass or clear
    perspex

You can sometimes see moths and other insects flitting around street lamps or porch lights, but if you have a light box, the insects will become trapped and you can examine them more easily.

Making a proper light box can be dangerous unless you know a lot about electricity, so it is best to ask your parents to make one for you, according to the following instructions. If no-one will help, don't worry, because you can use a powerful torch instead, as we shall see later.

To make the light box, you first make a hole large enough to take a lamp holder in the back of the wooden box. Screw the lamp holder firmly in place and insert the bulb. Then fix the two pieces of glass to the inside of the box with adhesive tape as shown. They should slope forward,

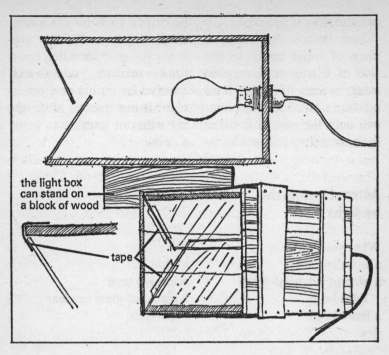

the light box can stand on a block of wood

tape

with the top piece overlapping the bottom and with a gap between the two pieces of glass of about $2\frac{1}{2}$cm. Don't worry if your pieces of glass are narrower than the inside of the box, just fill the gaps around the edges with strips of sticky paper. Your light box is now ready for use. Take it outside (unless you have a long flex you will probably need an extension lead if you are going to use the box outside) or secure it firmly to the open window of a darkened room and switch on the lamp. If you have no success at first, try changing the position of the light box so that it throws out light in a different direction. Inspect the box from time to time to see what insects are inside.

If you cannot get anyone to make an electric light box for you, make one yourself with a larger hole in the back of the box, and use a strong torch beam instead.

Looking at Flowers

A flower is the structure where the male parts (the *stamens*) and the female parts (the *carpels*) of a plant are produced. In addition the flower usually has petals and sepals. Later on, we shall see just what each part of the flower does.

You only have to look at the flowers in your garden, or those growing wild, to realise just how many different kinds there are. Perhaps the simplest way to learn about flowers is to study a common one such as a buttercup, and then to compare it with other flowers once you are familiar with the different parts.

Studying a buttercup

What you need
a safety razor blade or wood
    modellers' knife
a magnifying glass or hand
    lens
some fresh buttercups

First, note the five green sepals which protected the young, developing flower. Together the sepals are called the *calyx*. The buttercup has five bright yellow petals. At the base of the petals are nectar stores (nectaries) which attract insects to the flower. The ring of petals is called a *corolla*. Remove a petal and examine it with a hand lens. Note the honey guides. These help the insect find the nectar.

There are many stamens in the buttercup. The stalk of the stamen is called a filament and the *anther*, on top, produces pollen. There are also many carpels in the buttercup. Each carpel is made up of the *stigma*, the *style*, and

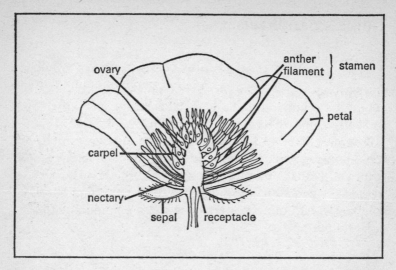

the *ovary*, containing many *ovules*. If the buttercup is carefully cut in half (ask a grown-up to do this for you), you can see how the parts are arranged around the *receptacle*. Make a drawing of your half-flower.

When a visiting insect comes to the buttercup to drink the sugary nectar, some of the pollen from the anthers sticks to its body as it brushes past. When the insect visits the next flower it brushes some of this pollen on to the stigma of the carpels. This is known as *insect pollination*, and it is the main method by which pollen is transferred from flower to flower. However, some plants, such as grasses, rely on the wind to carry their pollen from one flower to another.

Once the pollen lands on the stigma, it produces a tube called the pollen tube which grows down into the style and eventually into the ovule. In the end of the pollen tube is a tiny male nucleus which fuses (joins) with a female nucleus in the ovule. This joining of the male nucleus with the female nucleus is called *fertilisation*. In time, the fertilised ovule turns into a seed which will eventually grow into a new plant.

Studying other flowers

What you need
a razor blade
a magnifying glass or hand
lens

any common flowers (daffo-
dil, poppy, tulip, rose,
white dead nettle)

Look at any common flowers
(a few are suggested above) in
the way that you did for the
buttercup, and try and
identify all the parts.

Here are some questions to ask yourself when you are
looking at the flowers:
1. How many sepals and petals are there?
2. Are the sepals and petals different colours?
3. How are the sepals and petals arranged?
4. Do the petals form a tube?
5. Are all the petals the same shape?
6. What insects visit the flower?
7. Are both the male and female parts (stamens and carpels)
   present?
8. What are the stamens attached to? (Look very carefully
   at the base of the filaments.)
9. How many stamens and carpels are there?
10. Is the flower scented?
Note any other observations that you make.

What Do Insects Like to Drink?

Many insects, such as bees, visit flowers in order to drink the sugary substance called nectar which is usually produced in *nectaries* at the base of the petals. Whilst drinking this nectar they help to pollinate the flowers, as we saw earlier. The nectar is a sort of reward which the flower offers to the insect for visiting it. Other insects, flies for instance, are not so readily attracted by the sweet smells of nectar-producing flowers, and they prefer smells that we would find unpleasant, smells that are known as foetid.

This project is best done on a hot summer's day when there are plenty of insects in the air.

What you need
5 saucers or dishes all the
    same colour
coloured card
milk
water
sugar
salt
a small piece of rotting meat
paper
pencil

Place the five saucers in the sunlight, preferably near some flowers. A large piece of white, yellow or blue card placed under each dish will help the insects, but you must use the same colour under each dish. Fill one saucer with milk, put some jam on another, a little raw meat that is 'going off' on the third, some salt dissolved in water on the fourth and some sugar dissolved in water in the last. Remember which dish contains the salt water and which

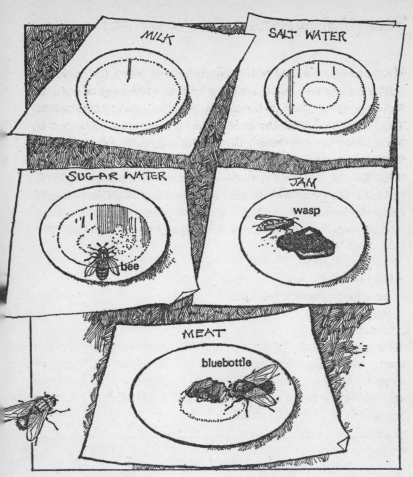

has the sugar water.

On a piece of paper write the words 'salt', 'jam', 'sugar', 'meat', 'milk'. Now sit quietly and see what insects visit each dish. Make a record of the number and note what sort of insects they are. After a short time you will be able to see which types of insect prefer which substances. Why do you think most insects, especially bees, prefer the sweet-tasting sugar and jam? Why are flies attracted to the meat?

61

Looking at Fish

If you have ever kept fish in an aquarium, you have probably noticed their streamlined shape, the way they use their tails for swimming through the water, how their mouths open and close, and so on. There is certainly an enormous amount to be learned by studying live fish but, equally, there is also much that you can learn by looking closely at a dead fish. This is best done as a two-stage process. Firstly, we shall examine the parts we can see on the outside of a fish (we shall use a mackerel here, but there are many others you can choose), and, secondly, we shall look at the parts inside the fish.

What you need
a sharp knife
   or a pair of small scissors
a small dead fish

You can buy a small fish from the fishmongers for this project; sprats are available in the winter, but other fish such as herrings or mackerel can be bought in the summer. Always buy an unfilleted fish (one that has not had its body organs removed).

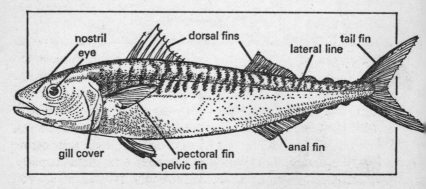

Lay the fish on its side on a board. How many of the parts shown in the illustration can you see? All the fins have special parts to play. The tail fin is powered by muscles running down the fish's body and it thrusts the fish through the water. The dorsal and anal fins help stop the fish rolling about in the water, and the pectoral and pelvic fins keep the fish level as it swims.

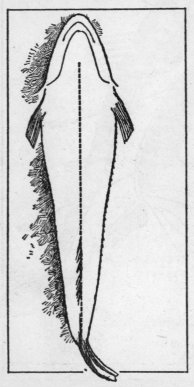

Notice how the skin is darker on the back than on the underneath. This darkness makes the fish hard to see when it is swimming near the surface, and helps protect it against hungry birds like gulls and herons.

The body is covered with scales. Running down the side is the lateral line which helps the fish 'feel' movements in the water. Notice the eyes, mouth and nostrils. Lift the operculum (gill cover) and find the gills, the fish's breathing apparatus. As the fish opens and closes its mouth, water enters and passes into tiny blood vessels inside the gills, where the oxygen which is dissolved in the water passes into the fish's blood. In this way fish obtain the oxygen they need to breathe.

Now let's have a look at some of the parts inside the fish. Make a cut through the skin along the path indicated by the dotted line. Be careful not to cut too deeply or you will damage the organs before you have seen them properly. Probably the first organ you will see is the roe. In the mating season the roe is very large and looks like two long, milky-coloured bags. Gently remove the roe and then carefully pull out the other body organs after noting their position in the fish's body.

The organs are lightly bound to one another by a thin, transparent substance called connective tissue, and you will have to pull them away from each other before you can display them like those in the illustration.

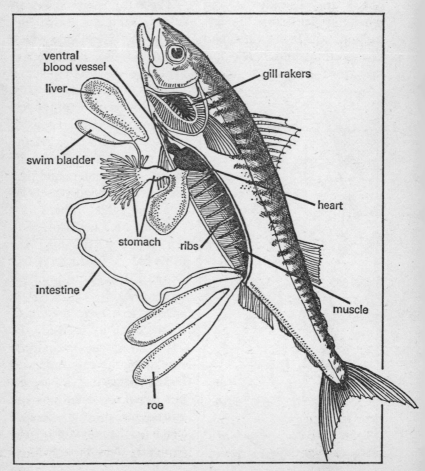

How Seeds Grow

Seeds are produced by many plants after fertilisation. They are the means by which plants can colonise new territory and carry on the species. In many ways, there are similarities between seeds and spores because both have similar jobs. If a seed lands in a suitable place, it usually undergoes a resting period, after which it begins to produce a root and a shoot. This is called *germination*. If conditions remain suitable for the growing seed, it will eventually turn into a plant just like its parents. Later on, we shall investigate the sort of conditions necessary for a seed to grow into a healthy plant.

Growing pea seeds

What you need
blotting paper
a jam-jar
water
a few pea seeds (i.e. peas)
   soaked in warm water

Pea seeds are the best kind to use because they germinate quickly and are easy to see, but you can use other seeds, such as beans, instead.

Cut the blotting paper so that it will fit neatly inside the jam-jar. Now carefully push four or five seeds between the blotting paper and the glass. (If you have soaked the pea seeds in warm water for a couple of hours first, they will germinate more quickly.) If the seeds keep dropping to the bottom, you will have to pack some shredded news-paper in the centre of the jam-jar (inside the blotting

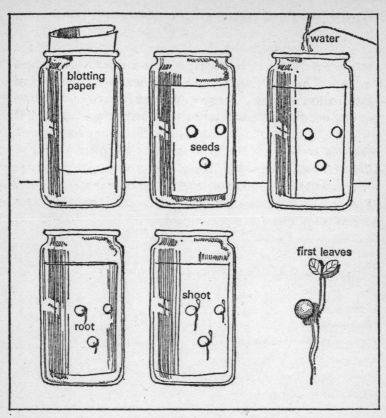

blotting paper

water

seeds

first leaves

root

shoot

paper ring) to wedge them. Now pour about 2 cm of water in the jar and stand it in a warm place. After a few days the seeds will start to germinate. First the *radicle* (root) appears and starts to grow downwards. Next the *plumule* (shoot) appears and, as it grows, it pulls the first young foliage leaves out of the seed. Whilst the young pea plant is growing, it receives its food from the *cotyledons*, a kind of store within the seed. Plants like the pea have two cotyledons and are called *dicotyledonous* plants. Grass seeds have only one cotyledon and are called *monocotyledonous* seeds. Most plants are dicotyledonous.

What do seeds need for germination?

We already know that light is not usually necessary for germination because most seeds germinate underground where it is dark. The right temperature, and the correct amounts of oxygen and water are necessary, however. Let us see what we can find out about these other conditions.

What you need
3 dishes with covers
blotting paper
water
pea seeds soaked in
    warm water

Take the three dishes, place some damp blotting paper in the bottom of each and put a few pea seeds on the blotting paper. Cover the dishes, and put one in the refrigerator or in a very cold place; put another in a hot place such as on a boiler or a hot radiator; and put the last somewhere where it is warm, but neither hot nor cold. After several days, compare the germination of each batch of seeds.

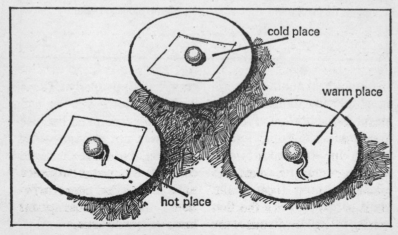

You should find that the seeds in the very hot and very cold places have not fared as well as those in the warm place. What does this prove? them and keep them in a warm place. In a few days you will find that only the seeds in the dish containing damp blotting paper have

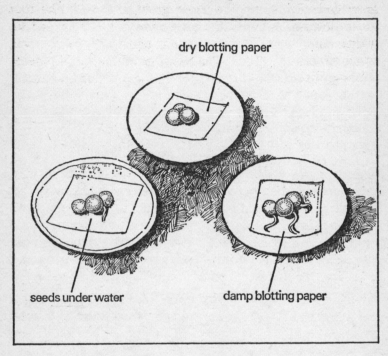

dry blotting paper

seeds under water

damp blotting paper

Now set up another experiment placing damp blotting paper in the bottom of one of the three dishes, dry blotting paper in the second and enough water to cover the seeds by about 1 cm in the third. Again, place a few pea seeds in each dish, cover germinated properly. Those with dry blotting paper will not have germinated because there was not enough water for them, and those that were covered by water will not have germinated properly because the water prevented them receiving oxygen.

Experiments on Young Shoots and Roots

Once the seeds have started to germinate, why does the root grow downwards and the shoot grow upwards? The root grows downwards because it grows away from light and towards water which, in the natural conditions of the soil, would be below ground. The shoot grows upwards because above ground it will find the light it needs for photosynthesis.

Can you make a root grow upwards?

What you need
a jam-jar
water
blotting paper
a few pea seeds soaked in
    water

shoot
root

Set up the experiment as you did when growing pea seeds.

When the root has just begun to grow out of the seed,

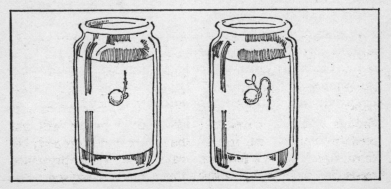

turn the seed upside down so that the root is pointing upwards. As it continues to grow, the root will bend so that it again grows downwards. Roots are affected by gravity and grow towards it; they are thus described as positively *geotropic*. Roots are also positively *hydrotropic*; in other words, they are attracted to water.

Can you make a shoot grow downwards?

What you need
a jam-jar
water
blotting paper
a few pea seeds soaked in
    water

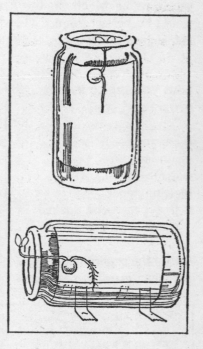

Set up the experiment in the same way once again. This time, ensure that the seeds are fairly near to the top of the jar. Once the shoot has started to grow out of the top, lay the jar on its side and prevent it from rolling around (a small piece of sticky tape will be sufficient). What happens to the shoot? It grows upwards and away from gravity. Shoots are said to be negatively geotropic.

Although the shoot is growing away from gravity it is also doing something else. It is growing towards the light it requires in order to produce its own food by photosynthesis. On the opposite page is another simple project to show how shoots grow towards light.

What does light do to cress seedlings?

What you need

2 cardboard boxes with lids (old shoe boxes are very suitable)
scissors

2 dishes
cottonwool
water
some cress seeds

Put some cottonwool in each of the dishes and moisten it with water. Now place a few cress seeds on each piece of cottonwool. Place one dish of seeds in one of the boxes and put the lid on. Cut a hole about 3 cm by 3 cm in the second box and put the second dish of seeds in it with the lid on.

Look into the two boxes after several days. (Don't open them before that.) The seedlings in the box with the hole cut in it will all have grown bending towards the light. Those in the box which received no light will be tall and thin, and have yellower leaves than those in the box which received light.

This shows that light makes the shoot grow more slowly but also helps the plant produce greener leaves. The green colour of the leaves is due to chlorophyll which, as we saw earlier, the plant needs to produce its food (photosynthesis).

On the following pages are more projects to enable you to study photosynthesis.

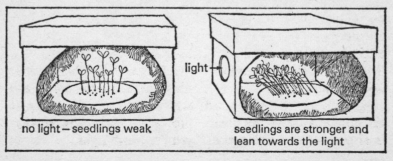

no light – seedlings weak

light

seedlings are stronger and lean towards the light

Experiments on Photosynthesis

The leaves of green plants are often thought of as the plant's 'factories', for it is in the leaves that most of the plant's food is produced by means of photosynthesis. The food made by the leaves is stored in the form of *starch*, but it is turned into sugar when the plant needs energy to build more cells and carry on its everyday functions. Therefore one of the ways in which we can tell if photosynthesis has taken place in a leaf is to test for the presence of starch. Iodine turns starch blue, and if you place some iodine on a raw, cut potato it will turn blue showing that starch is stored in the potato. (This also tells us that the leaves are not the only place where starch is stored.) We would not be able to see the blue colour of iodine-stained starch in a green leaf, however, so we must first wash the green chlorophyll out of the leaf to make it white.

Is starch present in green leaves?

heating methylated spirits

What you need
a saucepan
a small tin can
water
methylated spirits
iodine
a fresh green leaf

First, kill the leaf by placing it in boiling water for a minute. The leaf must then be placed in boiling methylated spirits to remove the chlorophyll. This can be a difficult procedure, so it is best if one of your parents helps you. It is very dangerous to try and boil methylated spirits

72

dip the leaf in iodine

alcohol, which boils at a lower temperature than water so the heat of boiling water is quite sufficient to make the methylated spirits boil.) When the leaf is placed in the methylated spirits it will begin to turn white as the alcohol dissolves the chlorophyll out of the leaf. Once the leaf is completely white, soften it by putting it into boiling water for a few seconds, and then dip it into the iodine. A blue colour indicates that starch was formed in the leaf as a result of photosynthesis.

directly over heat, but it will boil easily and safely when placed in a container which is itself placed in boiling water. (Methylated spirits is mainly

Is sunlight needed for photosynthesis?

What you need
a saucepan
a small tin can
water
methylated spirits
iodine

black paper and paperclips
adhesive tape
a fresh green leaf – still
   attached to the tree

We can easily prove that sunlight is needed for photosynthesis to occur by covering part of a leaf so that some of the leaf is in the light and some is in the dark. If we later test the leaf for starch, what should we find has happened in the part that was covered? We should find that starch has only been made in the part exposed to sunlight.

Cut the black paper into the shape shown and tape two of the edges together. Sandwich a green leaf, still on the tree, between the two pieces of black paper and, making sure that the paper is a tight fit over the leaf, use paper-clips as shown to hold it in place. The black paper will stop light reaching that part of the leaf. The paper should be placed on the leaf in the evening and left until the following evening. During the night, starch will have been taken from the leaf by the plant and used as food. As the leaf builds up more starch during the next day, no starch

should have been made in the part covered by the paper, because photosynthesis can only take place in the presence of light. After twenty-four hours, test the leaf for starch as you did in the first project. It should only be found in the uncovered part of the leaf.

Proving that oxygen is given off during photosynthesis

What you need
a jam-jar

a small glass funnel

a test tube

water

some pondweed

During photosynthesis, oxygen is given off by green plants. We cannot see oxygen, of course, because it is invisible. We can, however, collect it from a plant that is carrying out photosynthesis and test for its presence.

74

To set up the project, you will need to obtain some pondweed (*Elodea*). This grows in many ponds, but if you cannot find any, most aquarium stockists sell it very cheaply. Set up the apparatus as shown, with the weed in the jam-jar. It is best to rest the bottom of the funnel on two small coins or similar objects – this will allow water to pass freely. Place the jam-jar in bright sunlight. Soon, bubbles of oxygen from the pondweed will *displace* the water in the test tube and the level of water in the test tube will go down.

To test for the presence of oxygen, light a wooden taper and blow it out. While it is still glowing, quickly remove the test tube from the jam-jar and put the taper into it. The taper will relight with a 'pop', proving that oxygen is present.

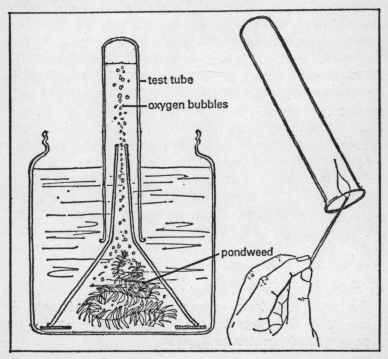

test tube

oxygen bubbles

pondweed

How Plants Take Up Water

Have you ever wondered how the water in the soil is taken up by plants? Water is, of course, very important because green plants combine water with carbon dioxide from the air (which enters the plant through tiny holes, called *stomata*, which are present in the leaves) to make their food. Water also acts as the transport system that carries food around the plant.

If you look very carefully at the roots of a green plant you may see tiny hairs near the ends. These are the *root hairs*, which are outgrowths of the outer cell layers of the root. These root hairs grow between the small soil particles, around which is a film of water. Now, although this water is really a solution of water and minerals (similar to a solution that you would make by dissolving some salt in a cup of water) its *concentration* – the strength of the solution – is weaker than that of the cell sap in the root hairs. In nature, the liquid from weaker solutions (remember a solution is liquid with materials dissolved in it) tends to pass through living cell walls and mix with stronger solutions. This phenomenon is knows as *osmosis*. The picture shows a section of part of a root in the soil. Just as the concentration of the solution of cell A (the cell with a root hair) was greater than that of the soil, so the concentration of the solution of cell B is stronger than that of cell A, because cell A has been made weaker by the extra water it now contains. Thus water flows into cell B from cell A, again by osmosis. In this way, water is drawn near the centre of the root, and by a variety of processes is gradually distributed through the whole plant.

root hairs

Osmosis in a potato

What you need
a dish
water
sugar
half a raw potato

Scoop out a cavity in the half-potato, taking care not to go right through. Place the potato in the dish containing some water. Now place a teaspoonful of sugar in the cavity of the potato. After three to four hours the cavity will be full of water and the level in the dish will have dropped. We have increased the concentration of the cells near the cavity due to the sugar dissolving into them, and this has drawn water from the outer cells and, eventually, from the dish itself.

Another demonstration of osmosis can be carried out by placing a ripe cherry in water. Very quickly, the outer skin of the cherry will split. This is because the sugary sap of the cherry draws in water and the cherry swells. The water has nowhere to go so eventually the skin just bursts. Is this why cherries on a tree often burst after rain?

What Happens to the Water in a Plant?

The water that a plant takes up from the soil in its roots passes up the stem and into the leaves, and eventually leaves the plant through the tiny pores, or holes, in the leaves called the stomata. This evaporation of water is called *transpiration*.

Showing that water evaporates from leaves

What you need
a large glass jar
some tin foil or
    plastic sheeting

a rubber band
a small potted plant

Cover the soil and pot with tin foil or plastic sheeting and secure it with the rubber band so that it is air-tight. Now place the glass jar over the plant and its pot. Soon, tiny droplets of moisture (water) will appear on the inside of the jar. Since the pot has been covered to prevent water evaporating from it or from the soil, the water must have come from the leaves.

Does the transpiration rate vary with temperature?

What you need
a large glass jar
some tin foil or
    plastic sheeting

a rubber band
a small potted plant

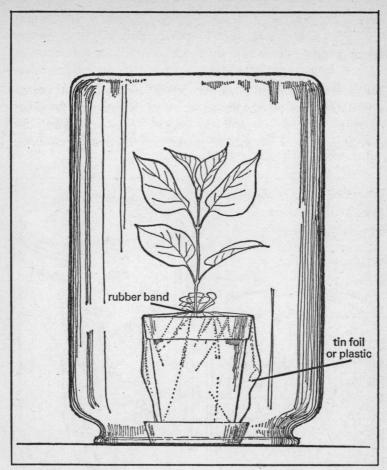

rubber band

tin foil
or plastic

Make sure that the soil in the pot is well watered – but not draining out of the bottom if there is a hole in the base of the pot – and again cover the soil and pot with tin foil or plastic.

Place the plant, with the glass jar over it, in a cold place. After a measured amount of time, note how much moisture is on the inside of the glass jar. Now completely dry the inside of the jar and set up the apparatus as before, but this time in a very warm place. (For the whole of this project try and use places where the light is constant). After the same length of time has passed, again note how much moisture is present. Alternatively, you could try the experiment first in a cold place and then in a warm place, and just note under which condition (hot or cold) droplets of water first start to appear.

What does this project tell you about the effect of temperature on the rate, or speed, of transpiration?

jar left in cold place

jar left in warm place

Birds

Birds are fascinating creatures to study. Their beautiful colours, their songs and their active way of life mean that we can discover much about them, sometimes by doing little more than just looking out of the window. Like most wild creatures, however, birds are shy and easily frightened, and two of the secrets to success when studying them are quietness and patience. It is no use tramping through a wood expecting to see lots of birds – they will have flown off in alarm long before you reach them. Instead, imagine you are a hunter, creep up on them slowly and stealthily, or sit quietly and wait for them to come to you.

The few projects in this book will help you begin your study of birds, but you may find that as your interest grows you will want to learn more. If this is so, join an ornithological society or local bird-watching group. The members always welcome enthusiastic young people and you will learn much from them. Also, there are probably more books about birds than there are about any other group of animals, so you have plenty to choose from if you want to find out about them.

The pictures here show some common British birds, but to identify birds properly, it is worth obtaining a field guide to the birds in your area. Good field guides are readily available

bullfinch

song thrush

pied wagtail

starling

and give useful information such as the areas where birds are found, and whether the bird is common or rare; also, they usually have pictures of the bird in flight, to help you identify those that are on the wing. It is worth saving up for a pair of binoculars (those stamped 8×30 are best), for they enable you to make a much more positive identification of birds at a distance. Identifying birds is probably more difficult than identifying animals in other groups because although the body shapes of birds vary, they do not differ as much as, say,

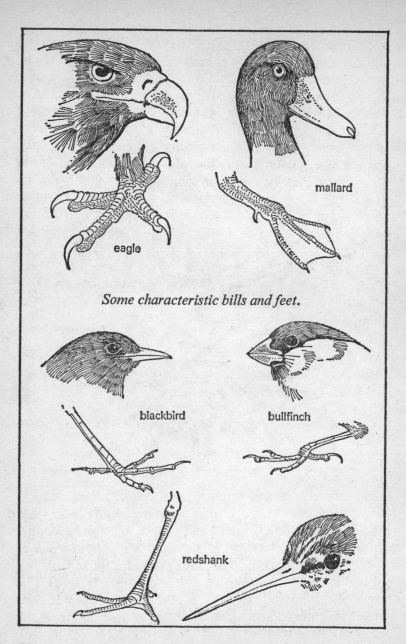

Some characteristic bills and feet.

eagle

mallard

blackbird

bullfinch

redshank

a whale and an elephant (both mammals). This is because all birds, except flightless ones such as ostriches, penguins and emus, have to be a certain shape in order to fly. They must have wings which can thrust them through the air, a tail to help them balance when flying and act as a brake when landing, and a streamlined body to cut down wind resistance. But there are, of course, many features which do help us identify birds, such as size, colour, the outline of the body, where they are found, how they fly, and their song. By looking at a bird we can often tell much about its way of life. The bill tells us something about how the bird feeds. For instance, a heavily built bill, like that of a bullfinch's, is used for eating seeds; the flat bills of many ducks are used for scooping up water weeds; the hooked beaks of birds of prey enable them to tear flesh from their victims; and the long, thin bills of many seashore birds allow them to probe into the sand and mud for food. Then there are birds such as thrushes and blackbirds with 'general purpose' bills for eating worms, insects and berries.

So what else can we learn about birds just by keeping our eyes open? There are many interesting aspects of bird behaviour that are easy to observe. Take singing for instance. Most birds sing during spring and summer. It is the male who sings and he does so to tell other birds that he has chosen a certain area as his territory, and also to attract a female for mating. Thus to an unmated female his song is a welcome, but to other male birds he is really saying 'keep out!' Watch a bird next time he is singing. He will usually perch on a chosen spot, perhaps a garden fence or in a tree, sing for a while and then move on somewhere else. These chosen spots, or *song posts*, mark the outer limits of his territory. If another male bird strays inside the territory it will be vigorously chased off. Try to identify the territory of a bird by watching him sing on his song posts. A note book is useful for jotting down the time of day he sings, how long he sings for, and so on.

Once a bird has chosen a mate, nest building begins. Nest

85

magpie

lapwing

sites vary from species to species but you may be lucky enough to spot a nest being built in your local wood or perhaps even in your garden. The birds fly backwards and forwards carrying suitable nest material – twigs, straw, feathers, mud, etc. – to the nest site. You can dangle suitable nesting material in a place where the birds can see it easily and see whether they take it and use it. Early spring is the time when most birds begin to build nests and a very enjoyable way of studying nesting is to provide a nest box or nest ledge.

86

mallard

grebe

oystercatcher

common gull

A nest for robins

What you need

2 pieces of wood 26 cm × 15 cm × 5 mm thick

1 piece of wood 15 cm × 18 cm × 5 mm thick

1 piece of wood 34 cm × 15 cm × 5 mm thick

2 pieces of wood 15 cm × 15 cm × 5 mm thick

some nails and a hammer or

some screws, a screwdriver and a drill

creosote

sealing compound

You can buy the wood quite cheaply from a timber store, where they will probably cut it into the correct lengths for you. Nail or screw the box together, following the instructions in the illustration. Use a sealing compound to fill any cracks so that the box is leakproof and draught-

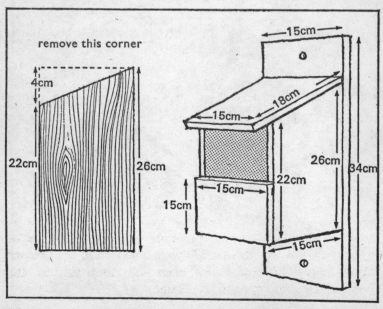

proof. Now creosote the outside of the box and allow it to dry. Nest boxes are best erected during autumn or winter. This will give them time to 'weather' and allow the birds to become used to them. The arch enemy of nesting birds is the domestic cat, so try and site the nest box where cats cannot easily reach it. Robins are not too fussy about how high the box is positioned – one and a half to two metres is satisfactory – but they like privacy, so try and conceal the box where it will become partly hidden by foliage. If you attach the box to a tree, wire it firmly in place, but do not use nails as these may damage the tree. If you are lucky, a pair of robins will use the box to build their nest in during the following spring, and much can be learned by studying the nest-building activities of the parents. Resist the temptation to keep looking in the box; an occasional visit for a few seconds when the parents are away will tell you how far things have progressed. Once the eggs are laid, you should

not approach the nest too closely if the hen is incubating them – she may become disturbed and abandon the nest. Write all your observations in your notebook – the date the nest was started, the date it was finished, how many chicks hatched out and when they left the nest. In this way you can compare the robins' nesting activities with those of other species. You may find, of course, that your special robins' nest box is used by another species of bird, but you can record their activities in just the same way.

A nest box for tits

What you need

2 pieces of wood 26 cm × 15 cm × 5 mm thick

1 piece of wood 34 cm × 15 cm × 5 mm thick

1 piece of wood 22 cm × 15 cm × 5 mm thick with a 2·5 – 2·8 cm diameter hole

1 piece of wood 15 cm × 15 cm × 5 mm thick

1 piece of wood 18 cm × 15 cm × 5 mm thick

a strip of old leather or canvas

some carpet tacks

an eye hook

a wood saw

some nails and a hammer

or

some screws, a screwdriver and a drill

creosote

sealing compound

The illustration shows you how to make the nest box. The position of the entrance hole is important, so try and ensure that it is positioned like this one. Weatherproof the box in the same way as you did for the robin nest box and hang it outside well before spring. You do not need to conceal the box in the same way as you do for robins, but remember to position it safely out of the reach of cats. The box can be nailed to a fence or a suitable post. Try to avoid siting it in direct sunlight; it is best if you can arrange for it to face north. An *occasional* peep inside the box can be made by lifting the flap, during which you can make observations to record in your notebook.

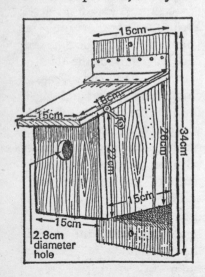

Other nest sites for birds

What you need
some old assorted pieces
  of wood
wire mesh or wire netting
nails
a hammer

Not all birds will want to build nests in boxes, but by erecting some simple platforms or ledges under the eaves of buildings you may be lucky enough to encourage house martins or swifts to build nests. The pictures show some simple ledges that can easily be made.

A bird table

During the spring and summer months there is plenty of natural food available for parent birds to feed their hungry young, but during the colder months of the year a simple way to watch birds is to provide food and water for them. This will not only attract them to wherever you place the food, but will also help them to stay alive when food is scarce.

There are several ways of feeding birds. You can simply scatter kitchen scraps such as bacon rind and bread crumbs, or hang up half a coconut – tits love pecking at these – or a small bag of mixed seeds or nuts. Perhaps the most rewarding way of feeding birds, however, is by making a bird table.

First of all, one end of the post must be made into a point so that it can later be pushed into the ground. Nail the four strips of wood on to the outer edge of the base to stop the food blowing away when it is windy. There should be a slight gap at each corner for water to drain away if it rains. Lastly, nail the base on to the top of the post. Some kinds of wood tend to split if you hammer nails straight into them, but if you ask your father to drill small holes through the wood first this will prevent splitting. The table should be placed where you can see it easily but where cats cannot creep up on the birds as they feed.

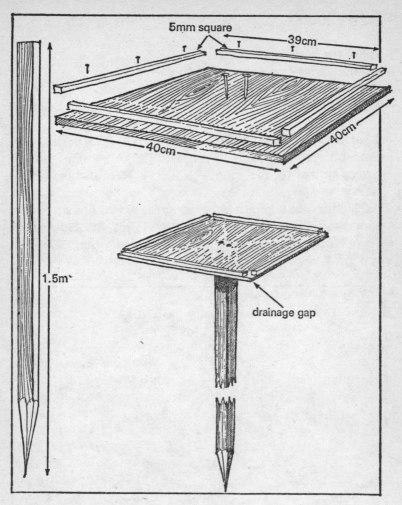

5mm square

39cm

40cm

40cm

1.5m

drainage gap

Try to observe the following and make notes in your book.
1. How long does each bird stay at the table?
2. Is one kind more dominant than the others?
3. Vary the food you put on the table. Are seeds favoured more than, say, bacon rind or bread crumbs? What do your observations tell you about birds' feeding habits?

Bird baths

What you need
an old baking tray or tin
some dry, sandy soil
water

Birds love to bathe. In fact, they become very unhappy if they do not get the opportunity to do so. Place a baking tray containing a little water on the ground and see what birds visit it to have a bath. Does the presence of one bird bathing attract others? Repeat the experiment using some sandy soil in the tray instead of water and note the results. How many types of bird bathe in this way?

Further things to do

Look for any bird feathers that may be lying on the ground. A magnifying glass will help you see how the feather is made. Try and find out the difference in structure and function between a *flight feather* and a *down feather*.

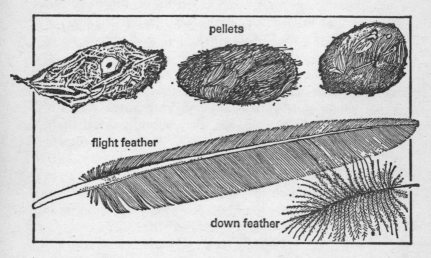

pellets

flight feather

down feather

An exciting find to look out for is a bird pellet. Birds such as owls and herons cannot digest certain parts of their prey – such as bones and feathers – and these parts are cast up as pellets. Owl pellets may be found in woods or old barns where owls are nesting, and heron pellets can be found along reedy riverbanks. If you carefully take the pellet to pieces, by first soaking it in warm water, you should be able to see some of the parts of the animals that went to make up the meal. Remember to wash your hands after handling bird pellets.

When you watch any kind of bird, make notes about the following: when it is on the ground does it walk, or hop? Does it jump into the air or run along the ground as it takes off? How does it fly: does it hover, soar, fly fast, slow, close to the ground or high in the sky?

A Year in the Life of a Tree

As the seasons change throughout the year – winter to spring, summer to autumn – so nature changes with them. During the cold winter months many animals hibernate because food is scarce, but during spring and summer life is at its busiest and the important business of rearing young is carried out while food is most plentiful. Plants, too, show a change in activity which is geared to the changing seasons, and this can be seen very easily in the deciduous (broad-leaved) trees.

In spring, the buds of the trees that stood like silent sentinels during winter now burst forth and bear leaves which will make food for the plant in the sunny months ahead. As the leaves on the trees continue to grow, so they provide food and shelter for the animals which live on them. Some animals, like caterpillars and squirrels, eat the leaves and fruit of the trees, but others, such as birds, come to the trees to feed on the smaller creatures to be found there. As the year continues and autumn approaches, many trees shed their fruit. Soon the leaves will fall, leaving only bare twigs and branches to sway in the winter wind.

In these projects we shall study the oak tree, because it is common and also because it provides a home for a variety of interesting animals – and other plants! If you do not have any oak trees growing near you, you can still carry out the following studies on other types of tree.

For most of the following projects the following general equipment will be useful: notebook and pencil, bags and bottles for carrying specimens in, a stick, an umbrella, some sheets of white paper, a magnifying glass, an insect identification book, coloured crayons and adhesive tape.

Wild creatures are easily frightened away, so to see the larger animals like birds and squirrels, which may be on the tree, remember always to approach quietly.

The oak tree in spring

Visit your chosen tree in early spring and draw a bud. Very soon, the buds will form leaves and the dangling catkins, which are really tiny flowers whose pollen is blown by the wind. There may be less to see than there will be in summer, so spring is a good time to make a bark rubbing (see page 23). Choose a piece of bark that is not too deeply pitted or furrowed. In your note book, record as many observations about your tree as you can – how high it is, how wide it is, and so on. The height of a tree can be estimated quite quickly and easily provided you have a protractor, a ruler, or other straight edge, a measuring tape and a set of mathematical log. tables (see page 99). First of all you have to know your own height (let us assume it is 1·5 metres). Now stand a measured distance from the tree, say 5 metres. Hold the protractor with its straight edge horizontal and level with your eye. Angle the ruler across the

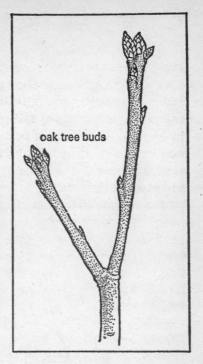

oak tree buds

protractor as shown until the far end of the ruler is in line with the top of the tree. Note the angle (say, 45°) that the ruler makes with the horizontal by reading it off from the protractor. Now, look up the tangent of that angle – let us assume it is 1. If you now multiply the tangent number by the distance you stood from the tree, and add your own height, the result is the height of the tree.

	tangent						
10°	0·1763	25°	0·4663	40°	0·8391	55°	1·4281
11	0·1944	26	0·4877	41	0·8693	56	1·4826
12	0·2126	27	0·5095	42	0·9004	57	1·5399
13	0·2309	28	0·5317	43	0·9325	58	1·6003
14	0·2493	29	0·5543	44	0·9657	59	1·6643
15	0·2679	30	0·5774	45	1·0000	60	1·7321
16	0·2867	31	0·6009	46	1·0355	61	1·8040
17	0·3057	32	0·6249	47	1·0724	62	1·8807
18	0·3249	33	0·6494	48	1·1106	63	1·9626
19	0·3443	34	0·6745	49	1·1504	64	2·0503
20	0·3640	35	0·7002	50	1·1918	65	2·1445
21	0·3839	36	0·7265	51	1·2349	66	2·2460
22	0·4040	37	0·7536	52	1·2799	67	2·3559
23	0·4245	38	0·7813	53	1·3270	68	2·4751
24	0·4452	39	0·8098	54	1·3764	69	2·6051

Example:

tangent of angle 45° = 1
multiplied by distance from
tree (5m) 1 × 5 = 5

plus your height (1·5m)
5 + 1·5 = 6·5 m
∴ the tree is 6·5 metres high

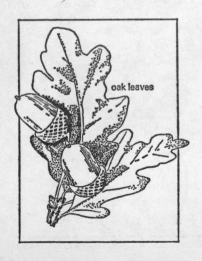

oak leaves

The width of a tree can simply be measured with a tape, getting a friend to hold one end for you if the tree is very large.

When the first leaves appear, make a leaf rubbing of one. Finally, make a coloured drawing of the oak tree in spring. If you have a camera and can take a colour photograph, that will be even better, especially if you are not very artistic!

The oak tree in summer

As summer approaches, the young oak leaves will have grown larger, and the tree will look very different from its bare winter outline. Sit patiently and you may see a squirrel running through the branches. Squirrels often build their nests in oak trees, eating the leaves and acorns (in autumn) as well as some of the smaller animals which live on the tree.

green woodpecker

blackbird

jay

Try to identify any birds which you find on the oak tree –
woodpeckers, jays and blackbirds are just three of the birds
you may see. Do any of the birds have a nest in the oak tree?

Perhaps one of the most interesting things about oak trees
is the insect life that abounds. Caterpillars may be found on
the leaves and twigs, and small insects in the crevices of the
bark. Look among the leaves, twigs and bark – using a magnifying glass if necessary – and record the names of all the
different insects you find. If you are careful, you will be sur-
prised at just how many tiny creatures are able to live on the
oak tree.

A useful way of finding insects among the leaves is to hold an open umbrella upside down under a leafy branch and shake the branch, or tap the leaves with a stick, to dislodge some of the insects, which will fall into the umbrella. You must quickly gather them up and put them into bottles so that you can identify them later. In addition to the animals that can be found on an oak tree, you may sometimes find other plants such as ferns, lichens, ivy and mosses which often grow on the trunk and branches of old trees. Plants

beating the leaves to dislodge insects and other small creatures

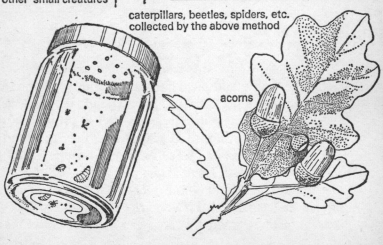

caterpillars, beetles, spiders, etc. collected by the above method

acorns

which grow on others are called *epiphytes*. Epiphytes are not like fungi – which are also plants that grow on others – because epiphytes do not actually use the tree as a source of food. If you have any epiphytes growing on your oak tree, what do you notice about their distribution? In other words, whereabouts on the tree are they growing?

In late summer the fruit of the oak tree appears. This is the acorn. Make a drawing of the acorn as part of your record of the year's study of the tree.

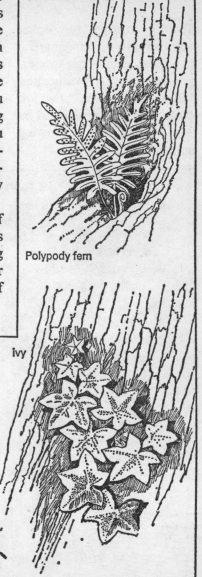

Polypody fern

Usnea – a lichen

Ivy

The oak tree in autumn

During autumn, the leaves will begin to turn from green to yellow, or in some species, red. Soon they will wither and fall from the tree, their job done, and will be replaced by new leaves the following spring. Early autumn is the time to look for fungi around the base of the oak tree, especially if the weather is warm but damp.

Try and see how many of the animals you found on the tree in the summer are still present.

The oak tree in winter

The oak tree will now have lost its leaves and will live on the supplies of food it made during the summer. Make a drawing of the oak tree in winter, or again if you have a camera, take a photograph, and compare this with the tree in summer. If squirrels are nesting in the tree you may be able to see their nest, or *drey*. You may even see them running about looking for food. Squirrels do not hibernate in winter, but for food they rely on the stores of nuts which they carefully hid away during the warmer months of the year.

The ground around the oak tree will probably be covered in dead leaves now, which, as they rot, will enrich the soil by forming humus. Bacteria in the soil will then turn this into new minerals for plants growing there. So although the leaves have finished their task for the tree, nature still provides a use for them.

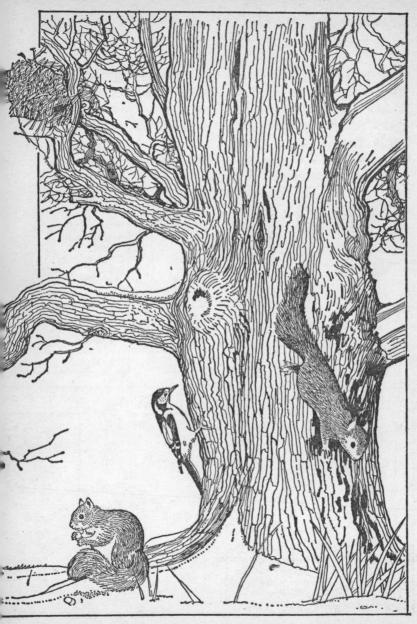

Displaying your study of the oak tree

The most satisfying way of displaying your study is to mount all the pictures, leaf and bark rubbings, and so on, on a large piece of card. The illustration shows one way of displaying your study, but you may well want to invent some other way for yourself.

OAK TREE IN SPRING

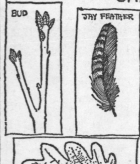

BUD

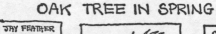

JAY FEATHER

BLUEBELL

ANIMALS
JAY
BLACKBIRD
WOODPECKER
SQUIRREL
CATERPILLARS
SPIDERS
INSECTS

NOTES
Height of tree ... 15 m
Location ..... Marckham Wood
Points of Interest

PLANTS
BLUEBELL
PRIMROSES

LEAF RUBBING

OAK TREE IN AUTUMN

ACORNS

ANIMALS   PLANTS

BULLFINCH FEATHER

FUNGUS GROWING AROUND BASE OF TREE: BRACKET FUNGI ALSO SEEN GROWING ON ROTTING BRANCH NEARBY

NOTES

ROBIN

BLUETIT

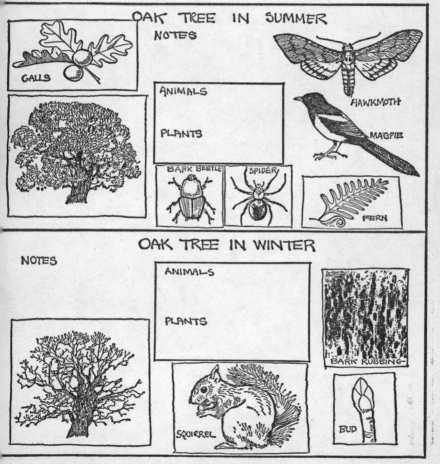

OAK TREE IN SUMMER

NOTES

GALLS

ANIMALS

PLANTS

BARK BEETLE

SPIDER

HAWKMOTH

MAGPIE

FERN

OAK TREE IN WINTER

NOTES

ANIMALS

PLANTS

BARK RUBBING

SQUIRREL

BUD

More Beaver Books

We hope you have enjoyed this Beaver Book. Here are some of the other titles:

Looking at Wildlife A Beaver original. Nicholas Hammond has written an invaluable guide for young naturalists, with lots of information on all kinds of wild creatures as well as advice on the best ways of observing them. Illustrated throughout

Lord of the Forest Written by 'BB' and with beautiful illustrations by Denys Watkins-Pitchford, this is the story of a mighty oak from its planting in 1272 until the last acorn from the dead tree is replanted in the 1939–45 war. A magnificent panorama of nature and history

My Favourite Animal Stories Sad, funny and exciting stories about all sorts of animals, chosen and introduced by Gerald Durrell

Buying and Keeping a Horse or Pony A Beaver original. The first of four titles in the Young Riders Guides series. This series gives all the information the young enthusiast needs to know about buying and keeping a horse or pony, caring for its health, feeding, riding and jumping. Written by Robert Owen and John Bullock, illustrated throughout with line drawings and black and white photographs

Animal Quiz A Beaver original. Johnny Morris, universally known and loved for his television programme *Animal Magic*, has created a picture quiz book about all sorts of animals, fish and birds, full of fun and fact for all the family

White Fang Jack London's great classic story about the life of a wild wolf dog at the time of the Gold Rush in the Yukon

New Beavers are published every month and if you would like the *Beaver Bulletin* – which gives all the details – please send a large stamped addressed envelope to:

Beaver Bulletin
The Hamlyn Group
Astronaut House
Feltham
Middlesex TW14 9AR

365891